CONTE

A Murmuration

Collected Poems by

Nick Wilde

DEDICATIONS

For my wife, Sue.

With grateful thanks to Walter, Simon and especially Tony

"I may disapprove of what you might say but I'll defend to death your right to say it".
Voltaire

"To understand everything is to forgive everything"
Attributed to Germaine De Staël

Cover photograph of a murmuration of starlings
by Nick Wilde
Cover design Tony Bostrom

Analogue Sound Storage Medium

You do know, don't you? You do realise?
We're not merely circles of polyvinyl chloride,
Shoved into tatterdemalion cardboard.
Oh no.
We are much more than that.
Much, much more.

'Well, you certainly don't look much,' I hear you say.
'Stacked in an old box,
Collecting dust in the Sally Ann charity shop,
Three for a pound.'

Past our best, I'll admit.
Gone is the brash arrogance of our youth,
Our glossy, contemporary swagger.

We're memories, and discarded ones at that.
Recollections of places and times gone by.
But mostly of people.
Of misplaced friends.
Of long enduring friendships.
Of loves found and long lost.
Of hurt and of happiness.

Analogue sound storage medium.

Somehow that description doesn't seem to do us justice, does it?

Not when you think about it.

We're a tiny piece of somebody's life.

So please.

When you hand over that pound,

Think about what it is you might be buying.

In The Zone

Pasty faced businessmen, ears jammed to a phone,
Shouting the odds as if they were alone.
Squealing brats, the pride of their mummy
Who is harassed and haggard, but still thinks she's yummy.
Tourists with cases who chatter and giggle,
Leaving the rest of us with no room to wriggle.
School-kids who frown and fidget their bums
As squeaks and explosions leak from under their thumbs.
Jabbering juveniles balancing frail plastic cups,
Sharing with all of us their downs and their ups.
Stroppy little tarts with brains made of porridge
And an attitude problem they refuse to acknowledge.
Pox ridden chavs who've crawled out from their drains
With the Neanderthal blood that runs through their veins.
Harvey Nics painted business women, munching their lunch,
Caressing their Apples, they have numbers to crunch.
Wearing my patience down to the bone –
'For goodness' sake people –
This is the Quiet Zone.'

The Ladies Hamilton

The Ladies Hamilton.

Their shop stands all sweeties and light.

One Mrs, two daughters.

No Mr?

A Tuck Shop trio.

Strong fingers for unscrewing lids from jars.

Measuring out pleasure.

Poppets.

Dolly mixtures.

Love hearts for the soppy.

Penny chews and sherbet dabs.

Or, if you are especially lucky, raspberry scoops of Lyons Maid
drowning in Corona lemonade.

Fizz and froth.

Jamboree bags full of mystery and temptation.

No father.

Two girls, one Mother.

Trick or treat?

Voices

'Guess what I found today?'

'What?'

'I said guess.'

'Give me a break, we are talking about the Cosmos here.'

'Do you remember that Galaxy I made, oh, eons ago now?
The Milky Way.
I was quite pleased with it at the time.'

'Can't say I do. Why?'

'I came across it when I was having a clear out.
It had fallen down the back of Space and Time.'

'So?'

'Well, here's the thing.
There's a bit of it - I called it The Orion Arm.
Purely for classification purposes.
Various planets and so on.

You wouldn't be interested.
Anyway.
One of the planets.
There's stuff growing on it.'

'Gross.
What sort of stuff?'

'I wouldn't like to say.
All sorts.
But what's really interesting is that one of these bits of stuff,
It's growing faster than anything else.
Destroying anything and everything it comes across.'

'Nasty!'

'You haven't heard the best part yet.
It is even destroying itself.'

'Now that is weird.
What are you going to do about it?

'Nothing.'

'Nothing?'

'No.

'I mean, why bother?

Who gives a shit?

The problem will solve itself.'

'If you say so, Dear.

Do you want any more of this Ambrosia?'

The Old Curiosity

The Ballad of Sprauncy Jauncy and Juicy Lucy

Sprauncy Jauncy met Juicy Lucy on their way to The Strawberry Fair.

Said Juicy Lucy to Sprauncy Jauncy 'Good heavens, what have you got there?'

Said Sprauncy Jauncy to Juicy Lucy 'Young lady, it's rude to stare.

And you should never approach a handsome young beau on his way to The Strawberry Fair.'

Juicy Lucy and Sprauncy Jauncy strolled on to The Strawberry Fair.

Sprauncy Jauncy said to Juicy Lucy 'You're possessed of a beauty most rare.'

Said Juicy Lucy to Sprauncy Jauncy 'Sir, my mother bade me beware.

But I'd fain take your arm, that can do no harm, as we walk to The Strawberry Fair.'

Sprauncy Jauncy and Juicy Lucy tarried long at The Strawberry Fair.

Said Juicy Lucy to Sprauncy Jauncy 'I've a thirst I do declare.'

Said Sprauncy Jauncy to Juicy Lucy ' To a hostelry then let us repair.

A glass of Rhenish, our strength to replenish, e're we depart The Strawberry Fair.'

Said Juicy Lucy to Sprauncy Jauncy
'The wine has gone to my head.'
Said Sprauncy Jauncy to Juicy Lucy
'You'd best rest for a while (*Aside*) on a bed.'

Said Sprauncy to Juicy
'You've captured my heart.
I think that I love you by Jove.'
Said Juicy to Sprauncy
'Sir my head's in a spin.
Would'st thou plunder my treasure trove?'

Said Sprauncy to Juicy
'You're a comely young thing,
A maiden both virtuous and pure.'
(*Aside*) 'But if I have my way, by the end of the day
The world will have one maiden fewer.'

Spraunce said to Juice
' I've drained my cup
I think it's time for a tup.
Said Juice to Spraunce
'You are forward sir,
And I'd venture no gentleman either.'
(*Aside*) 'A cheap glass of wine to make me feel merry
And the next thing you know he's after my cherry.'

Said Spraunce (*Aside*)
'Albeit she's chaste and would reject my charms
She will succumb to the power of the plonk.'

Said Juice to Spraunce 'I am virgo intactica
Or if your prefer the vernacular
I have yet to have had a bonk.'

Said J to S
'I should say no
But I'll give it a go.'

Said S to J
'Then let's have it away......'
Said J to S
'It don't 'alf make a mess.'

Juicy Lucy met Sprauncy Jauncy on their way to The Strawberry Fair.

Said Sprauncy Jauncy to Juicy Lucy, 'Good Heavens, who have you got there?'

Said Juicy Lucy to Sprauncy Jauncey, 'Once I had not a care,

Now I wish I'd not met a handsome young beau on his way to the Strawberry Fair.'

A Murmuration

Swirling and swerving
Tossing and turning
Accelerating, arcing
Rocking and rolling
Looping loops
Instinctive, inimitable
Nosediving
Gone

An English Rose

An ash tray crammed full with anger.

Rain, stinging the night, while shame stings the memory.

Headlights play peek-a-boo between cracked curtains,

Caressing discarded nylon, reflecting in dribbling water.

C & A cardigan spilt on the floor.

Peggy Lee on the radiogram.

A forlorn and loveless room.

Pesetas and The Children of Kodak pushed to the back of a drawer.

Were those the knickers?

Pirated by semantic overtures.

And now she lies alone in a cold, bracteal bed,

Nubile yet.

With memories of a lifetime, recollections of a day.

Dreaming, yet again, of the one that got away.

Yummy Mummy

I am a Mummy
And I am yummy.
I have another growing in my tummy -
A precious cargo, fruit of my womb.
I think that I might start a baby boom.

I have a hubby.
He's pink and chubby.
He does his bit, though he is tubby.
He likes to put buns in my oven.
Our aim is to beget a round half dozen.

I've always reckoned
That I was fecund.
I could pop one out at any second.
I squeeze them through my private runnel.
It sees more throughput than the channel tunnel.

When I go shopping
With my belly whopping,
A Waitrose aisle I will be blocking.
My pram has the beam of an ocean liner.
And more babies than there are in all of China.

If on the tube
I whip out a boob
Some people think this is taboo.
But I don't care if you think it's rude.
My darling new born Prince must have his food.

When I drink latte
And I'm looking tarty
You'd think it was a children's party.
I am so noisy - chitty chatty.
My grating voice is bound to drive you batty.

I am a Mum
And here I come
Twins in my buggy and then some.
If you find us in an elevator
It's probably best if you came back later.

Yes, she's a mater.
Thinks there's nothing greater.
And if you take against this germinator,
Please don't try to discommode her.
She'll run you down with her Range Rover.

The Scream of the Butterfly

It's blood, and cold black leather gloves
Clutched to a loveless bosom,
Fingers seeking out the fatal black hole,
Fearful eyes staring in disbelief at the dribbling away of life.
For your own safety.
Please - do not cross the dirty white lines.

It's discarded litter on the roadside.
Cans, plastic bags, rubbish from Ronald.
Excrement on footpaths.
Tears after bed-time.
Andersen turned Grimm.
The clothes of the emperor now visible but the emperor invisible
within.

It's dark after dawn
Awaiting the freedom of night.
Pained faces peer reviewed,
Scrabbling for passing pleasure,
Reaching for ectoplasmic mirages.
The magic of the silver scream.

Shared histories deleted.

For your own sanity.

Please.

Please do not cross the ugly grey line.

Hensal

This is the place I first felt the wind,
Jostling the tree tops aside,
Curling in and out of the branches.
This is the place where I first heard the rooks,
Wheeling, cawing, dancing.
This is the place I first looked at the sky -
The clouds, their shades, their warnings.
This is the place I first bathed in rain,
Drizzling, persistent, then pouring.
This is the place where I first met me,
Not yet knowing who me might be.

This is the place where I saw my first bluebells,
Conkers, beech nuts and acorns,
Falling to earth in due season.
This is the place I picked my first blackberries,
Stems scratching, stinging and staining.
This is the place where I first touched the primrose,
Pale yellow, shy and beguiling.
This is the place I first brushed through the wheat,
Shimmering, shining and glinting.

This is the place where I first met fresh birth -
Honey the Lab with her litter,
Licking, nestling and mewling.
This is the place I first poked at frogspawn,
Speckled jelly, new life forming.
This is the place I first met death,
Motionless, pale and bleeding.
This is the place I first thought of beyond,
Its space, its darkness and meaning.

This is the place where I first dug the soil,
Stubborn against the tine,
Found worms and slugs and snails.
This is the place where I first planted a crop
Needing water, sunshine and weeding.
This is the place where I first fed the earth,
The compost pungent and mouldering.
This is the place I first lifted potatoes
The brown earth sticky and clinging.

This is the place I raced my first horse,
Dappled grey and wooden,
Rocking, kicking, prancing.
This is the place I walked my first mile
Across stiles, along muddy footpaths.
This is the place I first rode in a car,
 Princess polished and gleaming.
This is the place I first floated a boat,
Yawing, pitching, then sinking.

This is the place where I built my first castle,
Crafted from the sands of Camber,
Fated to collapse in the tide.
This is the place I first smelt the sea,
Its weed, its greed and grasping.
This is the place I first collected shells,
Stuck to the beach, half hiding.
This is the place I played Ducks and Drakes,
Stones bouncing, jumping and leaping.
This is the place I first met me,
Not yet knowing that me would be.
This is the place where he met she.

The Office Party

He threw me a smile.
But I was wise to his guile.
He gave me a wink.
I flushed and turned pink.
As I drank my wine he practiced his chat-up line.
But he talked to my tits.
That didn't thrill me to bits.
He started patting my hand – said I looked grand.
Asked me to dance.
He thought he was in with a chance.
We danced slowly to the band.
I became aware of his gland.
He reached down for my rear,
His smile now a leer.
Next, he tried for a snog, but that was just the prologue.
Because he fondled my breast then groped for the rest.

When I sued for assault, it was all my own fault.
Turns out, I'd been gagging for a bloody good shagging.

Action Stations

Action stations! Action stations!
Beautiful babe alert.
Action Stations! Action Stations!
Tight sweater and short skirt.
Action Stations! Action Stations!
Wonderful eyes of blue.
Action Stations! Action Stations!
Wonderful thruppennies too.

As you were. As you were.
All operatives at ease.
As you were. As you were.
She's only trying to tease.
As you were. As you were.
She's with that ugly bloke.
As you were. As you were.
There'll be other fires to stoke.

A Centurion's Lament

I'd say unto one 'Go' and he'd goeth.
I'd say unto another 'Come' and he'd cometh.
And then it was said unto me 'Finito Benito'
Good night Vienna.
The Fat Lady has started to sing.

To bring home the bacon –
A time honoured station –
But the train has come to a halt.
Though not always gravy
It was at least savoury –
There must be a fault on the line.
Written out of the script, a hero eclipsed,
A star destined to fall and decline.

Or, maybe life begins at UB40?
Goodbye to motorway madness,
Farewell to leaves on the line,
Exchange my sandwich for a sand wedge,
Tend the garden, beg no pardon
Enjoy the Old King Cole.
'Would the next contestant sign on, please.
Here's some money for passing stop.'
A consolation for being a flop.

'To our requirements you are now surplus.
You are no longer fit for purpose.
Your password has expired.
You are about to be retired.
So log off, bog off and be gone.'

The Ballad of Cricklewood Broadway

The night Jack Green got bottled
All was placid and calm,
No evidence of disturbance
Nor need of the law's long arm.
The night Jack Green got bottled
He should never have come to harm.
But the boys in the public got fractious.
Well, it's part of their native charm.

It was windy and wet on The Broadway
Where Jack pounded his usual beat.
He was hoping the local rapscallions
Weren't planning to be indiscreet.
It was cold and wet on The Broadway
As he proceeded on plod plates of meat,
When he stopped outside of the boozer
To peer up and down the dark street.

Now inside the pub there was chaos
And already one body lay flat.
Forcibly struck by a pool cue
Which had been swung à la baseball bat.
Inside of the pub it was chaos
And though the beer was deemed to be gnats,
It was fair to say that the miscreants
Fled the scene in a state of pissed rats.

As Jack stood on the draughty street corner,
Dreaming of home and of bed,
A gang of jostling geezers
Knocked his helmet from off his head.
As Jack stood on that draughty street corner,
Just earning his crust of bread,
He made contact with a bottle of Guinness
And his consciousness he shed.

The bloke who did such grievous damage
(There's them that says he's a nonce)
On the fateful night in question
Clocked Jack a right bang on the bonce.
The bloke who caused such grievous damage,
Laid Jack low with such subtle nuance,
Was in front of the beak next morning.
Jack was hoping he'd be jailed for yonks.

Today is a Day

Today is a day for slouching behind restaurant wheelie bins,
Sheltering from the freezing wind,
Smoking a last cigarette,
Aimlessly prodding its expended companions with the toe of your shoe.

Today is a day for walking along the canal bank
Watching rain circles.
Kicking empty lager cans
And being careful not to dip your trainers into puddles.

Today is a day for standing at bus-stops
Soaked to the skin by persistent drizzle,
Not giving a shit about your exam results
And being splashed by the number 13 that doesn't even bother to stop.

Today is a day for cowering in a station café,
Spooning a Yum-Yum crumb from cold coffee,
Poking a thumb at your phone,
Hoping that no-one will come and sit next to you.

Today is a day for crouching on the steps of a chip shop,
Contemplating the cracks in the pavement,
Warming hands on the friendly packet
And hoping that this time the salt has reached the bottom.

Today is a day for sitting in public lavatories
Smiling at the dates on the wall,
Feeling faintly sick
Then swearing because the paper has all gone.

Today is a day for going to the flicks,
Buying a snack to match the one covering the floor.
Wanting to include the noisy couple behind you
In the blood bath Quentin is running on the screen before you.

Today is a day for losing 3-0 at home,
Squirting Tommy K down your new home strip,
Wondering about who exactly is responsible
For deciding who is worthy of a pre-match silence?

Today is a day when all others seem the same.
When all same seems senseless.
A day when the future gapes aching in front
And the past chases remorselessly behind.

Trompe L'œil

A phantom, deep in the abyss.
Barely awake, yet seeking escape.
One way or another.

Lamplight, spectral.
An evil eye in the security of surrounding night.

Black water, bottomless,
Motionless,
Staring at a sliver of silver,
Patiently waiting for another victim -
For another x-spectral existence.

Outside the Everyman, everyman is someone else inside his head.
Inside The Holly Bush.
Spilt beer and spoilt lives.
All the usual pub games.
While somewhere, out there,
Beneath the moon,
In the cold,
A ghost is giving up.

The Bethlehem Blues

Self-deprecating teachers on tip-toe, delicately gesticulating 'just so'.

Fashioned into a bespoke disguise, they weave and wobble on parquet.

There to present their matinee.

Conceived to what end?

An antiquated ritual bringing pleasure to Mum and Granny.

Lights, phones, action – let the show begin.

Angelic faces stumbling through artistic paces.

Mummy and Gran are entranced

As mumbled monotones dribble across the room in the 4 o' clock afternoon gloom.

Joseph, wooden as a Grecian gift.

A truculent inn keeper.

Plastic Jesus swaddled.

A coddled virgin, teachers' pet no doubt.

Shepherds and a glittering cardboard star.

No sunlight this night.

And wise men.

Sans cars, taxis or scooters with hooters.

Gaspar's tea towel is askew and he seems to have lost his frankincense.

Balthazar is fidgeting and sniffing.

Must be the myrrh.

Melchior, on the other hand, is being as good as gold.

He's been incentivised.

And then, suddenly it's all over.

A scraping of tiny plastic chairs.

Raking around in handbags for keys.

Herding the kids home,

Some via The Golden Arches.

Telling Dad all about it when he arrives home from work.

He pretends to be interested.

Don't Get Me Started

It stands squashed between the charity shop and Greggs.

A small newsagent.

A few locals still go there.

The old man who runs the place has cancer and they say he won't live very much longer.

His wife died years ago.

But then nobody liked her.

I don't think even he did.

Rumour has it an estate agent is going in.

His father started the business.

He was killed on D-Day.

Run over by an ambulance on the Finchley Road.

He'd sold all the usual stuff.

Newspapers and comics.

'Bring back The News of the World, that's what I say.'

And who could forget Lord Snooty and his mates?

And then there were the paper rounds.

How do you get up so early every day of your working life?

Weekends included!

Nothing but inky fingers and cold, stewed tea for breakfast.

Remember the small army of kids needed for deliveries?

Shoving wads of words through gagging letterboxes.

Sundays were the worst.

All those colour supplements.
Parents won't let their kids out alone these days.
Can't say I blame them.
What is the world coming to?

Mustn't forget the cigarettes.
'Wally Grouts' my Dad called them.
(You could get a packet of 10 in those days.)
Senior Service, Embassy and the like.
Not to mention the Golden Virginia, Old Holborn and Rizlas.
Useful things Rizlas.

Fireworks for November of course.
Catherine wheels.
Rockets, bangers and jumping jacks.
Crackers for Christmas.
Caps for six guns.

Ah well!
Time to close.
Nip into Tesco Metro for a pizza.
Maybe a Bud for a treat?
Pizza and Budweiser.
Who'd have thought?
This is north London, not the Upper East Side.
Don't get me started.

Switzerland

I'm saving up for Switzerland.
It's an awfully expensive flight.
No, I don't mean the one from Gatwick.
I mean the one into eternal night.

I'm checking all my body parts as they deteriorate in haste.
Each and every morning I'm scared to look below my waist.
My body is decaying in various varicose hues -
A good deal less of rhythm now, but a lot more of the blues.

The upper part's no better, it's turned to rag on bone -
I can't remember when it was my muscles last had tone.
Some people say my hearing's poor. (I play my music loud.)
But some people say I've hair galore. (Of that I'm rather proud.)
Sometimes my brain needs to re-boot, it switches off then on.
All the cells come flocking back, but a lot of the RAM has gone.

Talking of gone.
I can't go on and on.
Forever.
So what will happen when I fade?

When I can't turn up on parade. Slipping.

No longer in good Nick.
Perpetually on the sick.
I'll be a burden and a chore.
They're making old age against the law.
Will I sing as I suffer?
Just another ill old buffer.
Into obsolescence slowly sliding.
The final shunt to my last siding.

The National Health is bleeding death.
Who'd have thought they'd still have their leeches?
If you asked them to mind a place making beer
They'd probably fill their breeches.
Allowing the living to rot on the vine
But making the dying somehow divine.
Those at the coal face shouldn't share the disgrace,
They work hard in spite of disorder.
But the guys at the top who are running the shop,
They are well out of order.
Waiting lists as long as the Nile,
Targets to hit - with bows and arrows.
Processes flawed, common sense ignored,
Politicians in a state of denial.

It's not so much the getting ill,
It's the prospect of wasting away.
Living in a care home cupboard day after day after day.
I could buy a cut-throat razor and saw through a pulsing vein.
I could swallow a pile of pilfered pills and never swallow again.
I could jump from Beachy Head, but I don't fancy the splatter.
I could hang from the old oak tree until I'm mouldering matter.
I could buy a length of hose and lock the garage door,
Or walk into the sea and never be seen more.

Each of us owes God a death,
Or so The Bard once said.
Will stunned surprise catch my last breath,
Will I be in my own chosen locus?

How to manage those final phases?
With medical hocus pocus?
Where will I be when I go to blazes?

I'll probably go to Switzerland.
Don't you think that would be the best?
I'd hate to make a dreadful fuss
Just to find eternal rest.

I'll bugger off to Switzerland,
That land-locked Shangri-La
Where people go to die in peace
And shout their last 'Hurrah!'

I'm saving up for Switzerland,
The land of milk and honey,
Where I could die with dignity
If only I had the money.

Pitts

Pitts, Pitts, I loved you to bits,
Especially your broken biscuits.
And I loved your jam,
Your slices of ham,
Your tins of powdered custard.
A grocery store from the days of yore,
The flagship of our high street.
But if you came back today,
I'm afraid to say,
You wouldn't cut the mustard.

Pitts, Pitts even now your name sits
In the pantheon of the great emporia.
Your shelves of comestibles,
Sundry digestibles
And a trove of products domestic.
Bright tins of Brasso, packets of Omo,
A selection of cleaning necessities.
But the years have passed by
In the blink of an eye.
We've even gone and gone metric.

Pitts, Pitts you came to a stop.

The wheel of time overtook you.

Now your food's artisan,

It's a quiche not a flan.

That's a cornichon, not a gherkin.

Your selection's organic, additives are satanic,

Cakes are baked gluten free.

Yes, the magic has gone,

Your day is done -

So now you've turned into The Pumpkin

Aftermath

Gurneys in car parks
And strung out clinicians.
Overworked nurses and too few morticians.
Illegal hugging and redacted lives.
None of these things should come as a surprise.

De facto internment.
Civil rights in retreat.
Desperate families with no ends that meet.
Crashing world markets and ten pounds worth five.
None of these things should come as a surprise.

Inner city riots.
And blue suited zealots.
Floundering MPs and purposeless prelates.
Emergency measures more worldly than wise.
None of these things should come as a surprise.

As your fear grows.
When resolve fails.
When there's no remedy left to be had.
You're bound to remember your favourite things.
And then you will feel so sad.

Gurneys in car parks.

And strung out clinicians.

Overworked nurses and too few morticians.

Illegal hugging and redacted lives.

None of these things should come as a surprise.

Winnie The Poo

In matters scatological

This question is rhetorical.

Are bears indeed the species

That fill our woods with faeces?

Martyr

Sainted sinners
They lie at holy rest
To have pilgrims make their journeys,
To help nuns to keep their vows,
To give tourists something to do when it rains.

Be they stone faced in a secluded sepulchre
Or strangely effulgent in a stained glass window,
They stir in the reverent their piety and pity.
Such great men.
Such fine Christians.
Surely the Lord was with them?
How else could they have withstood the suffering?

The searing agony of burning flesh.
The choking smoke of Inquisition.
Taut sinew and cracked bone.
Blinded eyes and fingerless hands.
Faithful unto to death.

Inspiring yet more killing for the love of God.
For the love of God!

Prejudice and Pride

Breakfast, lunch and dinner, I really should be thinner.
I want to be much slimmer, breakfast, lunch and dinner.

Fish, chips and peas, some things come in threes.
My chin is one of these, fish, chips and peas.

Walnut, carrot and cherry, I blame Mary Berry.
I've the beam of a cross channel ferry, walnut, carrot and cherry.

Cappuccinos with chocolate chips, they barely touch my lips.
They rush straight to my hips, cappuccinos with chocolate chips.

Cabbage, potato and wurst, I eat 'til I'm fit to burst.
My stomach thinks it's been cursed, cabbage, potato and wurst.

Wine, whisky and scrumpy, why am I always so grumpy?
Is it because I'm always so dumpy? Wine, whisky and scrumpy.

Morning, noon and night the flab I have to fight.
People say I look a fright, morning, noon and night.

A smile, a hug and a kiss. Does my bum look big in this?
Oh, isn't it just bliss, when you get a smile, a hug and a kiss?

Scones, butter and jam, I'm happy the way I am.

I couldn't give a dam. So I eat scones, butter and jam.

Bouncy, buxom and big, I no longer give a fig.

Though I'm the size of a North Sea rig, I'm proud to be bouncy, buxom and big.

Lament for a Beanpole

I can't think of how to begin,
So I'd best cut straight to the chase.
You see, I don't take up very much space.
It's an awful thing to be thin.

There's more meat on a butcher's pinny
Than between this skin and these bones.
I could do with some extra stones.
It's a terrible trial to be skinny.

You can play Beat the Retreat on my ribcage.
My genes must be having a laugh.
I've the legs of a starving giraffe -
They're the size of Mr Hornby's OO gauge.

It is a dreadful fate to be slight.
The unkind call me scrawny.
How I wish I could be more brawny -
In a strong wind I'm prone to take flight.

I work hard on my calorie intake.
Thank heavens for the Great British Bake Off.
But no matter how many cakes I scoff
I still have the girth of a rake.

I'm as flimsy as a stick of wet celery.
I can pass through an eye, like a camel.
I've the depth of a coat of enamel,
And as narrow as the red line military.

There were those who would call me The Stick,
Draw comparisons to a twig.
I tried not to give a fig
But to be honest it got on my wick.

I weigh as much as a piece of confetti,
Gossamer-like on the scales.
I want to have blubber, like whales.
So I force feed myself with spaghetti.

There might have been no Eureka
Had I been Archimedes' guinea pig.
The displacement is not nearly so big
If you possess a body that's sleeker.

I resemble Mr Shakespeare's Cassius,
Lean and hungry to behold.
The fact is I've often been told
That there is nought to choose between us.

I'm as slim as an anchorite's diary,
Yet my fate could be so much the worse.
Being thin's not such a terrible curse.
It is merely that I am wiry.

Wendover Pond

Florence, Florence, Florence.

My parents named me Florence.

I expect they loved me truly

When they had some love to spare.

But I wasn't born to gladness,

To joyful celebration.

I was another mite to christen,

Another soul to save.

To clothe in care worn hand-me-downs.

Another mouth to feed.

No matter how the family worked

Ends would not meet each other.

 I was taught to take my solace

In the world to come.

To place my faith in gentle Jesus,

To worship and adore.

For his wondrous love and sweet compassion,

Would be mine forevermore.

Each and every Sunday I prayed for my redemption,

And each and every night I wrung my hands in my despair.

Then came the day my future arrived.
My life and death determined.
I was sent away to scivvy, sent away to slave,
To work my fingers to the bone.
To labour the live long day.
Beds to change.
Linen to wash.
Steps to scrub and hearths to blacken.
Silver to polish.
Collars to starch.
Curtsies to be curtsied.
Little Polly Flinders living life below steep stairs,
With an anvil in my heart and a void within my soul.

Because I couldn't bear the loneliness,
The exile from my home.
Hardship drove my days
And exhaustion cloaked my nights.
Another lamb of Jesus full of care and sorrow.
Another child of God trapped in a chasm of despair.

Flossie, Flossie, Flossie.
My parents called me Flossie.
But nobody prayed for Flossie when they heard I'd passed away.
I died alone, I died afraid,
With no prospect of a hallowed grave.

St Mary watched with righteous wrath,
Tolled 'It's a wicked thing you've done child,
A sin against both man and God.
A heinous, shameful crime.
For you there is no redemption,
No seat at God's right hand.
You'll not gain entrance to heaven, my child,
You are forever one of the damned.'

I was plucked from the arms of Jesus
By a vengeful and spiteful God.
No angels' wings for me that day.
If angels there were, they looked away.

So should you stare into the waters,
The waters of Wendover Pond,
Spare a thought for poor drowned Flossie,
Floating in the vast beyond.

Direct Debit

And then, quite unexpectedly,

Without so much as a 'by your leave',

The Sandman turns up.

Only this time with a cartload of earth.

Great clods of the stuff.

Wet and heavy.

And you think,

'This can't be right?

There must be some mistake.

Wrong address.

An administrative error.

A software glitch.

But Mr S is insistent.

Dumps the lot on your doorstep.

So you get to thinking.....

And there it is.

It's been staring you in the face all this time.

'How could I have been so stupid?'

Not out of sight, but definitely out of mind.

Not a contract as such.

Nothing in writing of course.

No guarantees or extended warranties.

A one off payment.

Place and time non-negotiable.

Back to School

Season of mists and rotting fruit.

Leaves on tracks.

The first steam of approaching winter rising from early morning platforms awash with cups of scalding coffee.

Only Christmas to look forward to now – as if.

That, or a sun seeking wait in an airport lounge – fat chance.

Capricious peddlers.

Helmeted, high vizzed, heads down, cutting through wind and pedestrian alike,

Wrapped against impending chill.

A light that flickers but is anyone at home?

The light is red – but better red and dead than green.

Odd that.

Back to school persons.

Care worn decorations of a long faded expectation.

Soiled.

Lead poisoned.

Love damaged.

Slouching petulantly by bus shelters or falling ungratefully from a travelling womb,

Clinging to devices as if their lives depend upon it.

Scrambled synapses will put paid to those and much else besides.

Fingers and thumbs engineering words – nil by mouth.

Computer degenerated.

The wheels on their bus go round and round

But the wheels within wheels are letting them down.

None too gently either.

Damp dusting windscreens.

Spray and mud smear,

Drivers crawling alongside kerbsides

Tracking an isobar to their daily depression.

Windows cracked to let out anxiety and an ersatz cloud of smoke.

Harrogate, Brighton et al.

A smug thought for every day.

Train fares up and markets down.

Or a blathering in the ears.

Banal, inane.

Let's hear what Little Miss Fatuous has for us today.

Traffic heavy heading into town.

Really?

Tell us something we don't know.

Preferably coherently, if that is not too much to ask?

You'd think they'd never been this way before but they'll be this way for evermore.

Lines of endless traffic slithering along greasy tarmac until the first frost kills more than the dahlias.

D.O.A.

I am not.
From then until now.
And henceforth.
Neither allowance nor allotment.

A split infinitive.
Expectantly fashioned into shape.
A ghost in a womb.
Spliced at the main brace.

Sugar pink turns cherry red.
Poppy blossoms from primrose.
Patent, pearl.
Neatly packaged for death.
Love born still.
A parody, a photograph,
A wanna be in a gallery.

Born of a desire to beget
What exactly?
Non modo sed etiam

Sylvia Andrews

1

Was it meant to be
When you met Henri
On that dismal London day?

Was there a frisson
When Cartier-Bresson
Boarded your omnibus?

You passed through fame's portal.
His lens made you immortal.
Ticket Inspector Andrews.

2

Did you go straight home that day?
Or to a rendezvous perhaps?
A tryst.
Maybe in Kensal Rise?
A weekly treat of lust.
An injection of spice.
A crumb of comfort.

Were you just the ticket or did you miss the bus?
Did you swing into the sixties,
Burst into psychedelic technicolour?
Or hide in the monochromatic shadows
Of London's greyscale winter uniform?
Did you ring the bell to get off,
Or ride a full route
To arrive at a sought after terminus?

3

There once was a woman called Sylvia.
Henri captured her in his camera.
As a result of that snap
Fame fell into her lap,
Shed light into her obscura

I'll Go No More A Roving

My days traipsing over Dartmoor are done.
I no longer view the pastime as fun.
I'd rather pass my time in the sun.
Simply relax in the old currant bun.

God save me from cold wet Welsh peaks
Where the view's unremittingly bleak.
Where the driving wind chafes my cheeks
And leaves my extremities frozen for weeks.

I've stopped walking the Derbyshire Dales.
I'm bored with their picture book trails.
For some reason their tracks now fail
To keep me both hearty and hale.

And as for the Dales of North Yorkshire,
And of this I am definitely quite sure,
I shall eschew their delights for evermore.
They make me so weary and footsore.

I avoid anything beginning with Ben.
I never want to climb one again.
They are just as hard to descend.
Leaving me yearning for a Lincolnshire fen.

So what of the District of Lakes
Where I've made many map reading mistakes?
Where there's Jenning's and Kendall Mint Cake.
Two treats I would gladly forsake.

Even Dunstable Downs have their tricks
Not least of which are the tics.
If to the back of your leg one should stick
You may well join the ranks of the sick.

Don't talk to me of Northumbrian hills.
There's many a Jack with their Jills
Who've experienced their wintertime chills
And cursed Messrs Wainwright and Grylles.

Beware paths that are beside the sea.
They take no note of the flight of the bee.
They're not helpful, directionally.
They are in, and then out, like MCCC

I once explored, with a friend, down under.
It turned out to be quite some blunder.
Nasty leeches our blood did plunder.
Tried to prise our bodies and souls asunder.

I've already walked far too far
So I think I'll just sit here in the bar
Peacefully quaffing a jar
And contemplating the descent of my star.

Sweet Iscariot

There is a ghostly pathway
Through the graveyard to the dark
Where the pallid mists of autumn
Caress the ghosts of love unborn –
Where shadows watch for snowfall in
Bluebell woods grown winter black
And listen for the footsteps
That are never coming back.

A Spinster of this Parish

A spinster of this parish.

Hardly a flower of Christendom.

Small, if not at all, breasts

Cower beneath acrylic and beads.

Dripped, dried seeds.

Child-bearing sighs.

Pure in word and deed if not thought.

Altar rail penitent,

Lips quivering on tip tongue.

A silent confession escaping unexpectedly.

Uninvited.

From a tangled chain of guilt.

A supplicant of fear for favour.

A waiver to be surely granted?

Passive on God's house maiden's knees,

Frantically, desperately seeking the comfort of ritual.

To savour at least something.

Praying to a pantomime genie.

Clasping a silver goblet, a gift from the devil.

Dribbles and drools.

A sheep in a meadow.

Surplus to requirements.

The Rising Sun

A setting sun squints over Bodmin, winking at a rising disk of tin.

The changing of the guard.

Conspirators of old.

In Altarnun, a Rising Sun.

Another evening dawning over bottles, glasses and cutlery, shiny bright.

To welcome travellers.

Unravellers.

Revellers for one night.

Grizzling bundles of pink, fractious children, tethers approaching their end after a long day in the car.

Or on the beach.

Trip advised, booking wise, from England and beyond, of a commodity to be traded.

Bar staff juggling customers and smiling through their irritation.

The punters want so much to fit in, to be part of it, one of the crowd.

But in the public they are inspected by and rejected by

Big Jack Horner, sat in his corner, drinking his pint of Tribute,

Declaiming and complaining to his pals about the grockles.

Farmer John, searching for an eye to catch,

His brow as furrowed as his fields.

He has a daughter behind the bar.

She has an admirer, smitten, bitten by the bug of love,
Desperate for a word of encouragement to garnish his pie and pint.
There is a shepherd, on Saturday night R & R, one dog, no collar.
Sipping half of lager, one of Trelawney's brood.
Bemused by the surrounding rebellion,
Ensconced by a grate as black as Newgate's Knocker
Stacked with cold fire.
Not quite knowing the reason why.

The unravellers have come to find themselves, to work down the
pasty mines,
To toil in the scone foundries
Or scrape together a bankruptcy selling tie-dyed skirts and surf
boards,
Homemade jewellery and such like tomfoolery.
Away with the fairies, with Merlin, Arthur et al.
Wanna be Guineveres attended by their knights in shining anoraks.

Bobby Dazzle on the razzle
Cutting a dash, flashing the cash.
A winning smile for the pretty maids all in a row, girl friends, who
might, or might not, enter into the spirit of things.
Still, nothing ventured.
Pies, pasties and chips, mushy peas and vinegar.
Veneer of grease on slippery lips,
Elbows stuck on anti-bacterial sprayed tables.
Cries of 'Scampi?' Deep fried.

The banging of stools, the clatter of pool

And the slops and pink kisses on glasses.

Fat arses shifting ill-distributed weight.

Drunken discourses as fingers, unwashed from the bog and with dirt under nails,

Plunge into shared packets of crisps.

Passing ships under sail,

Optical collusions, momentary imaginings,

Grist to the mill for the gristle that thrills.

And outside the wind carries the cackling and cursing of witches,

While the ancients look down from the moor and wait patiently for their time to come again.

Just Suppose

There is no god, of course.

But just suppose there is.

And not a god of love

But a god of indifference.

Just suppose we were created on a wet Wednesday in eternity.

As a sort of cosmic computer game,

Points for suffering and death.

And then god became bored and went off to play with other toys.

Just suppose.

The Front Bedroom

There is a secret here, hiding in the dark.

Where fingers claw at the bars.
Where crying is not allowed.
Here.
In prison.
Swaddled and suffocated.
Where it is not safe to reach outside.

There is a memory here in the dark.

Quickly.
Draw the curtains.
Shut out the moon.
Hide in the night.
Play pretend.
Hold on tight to Mr Bear.

There is a danger here in the dark.

And no one must know.
Mr Sandman comes this way
To banish Daphne's comforting voice.

Clippity clop clippity clop.
Is his horse a dapple grey?
No, just a worn out nag
Hauling its cart-load of yellow grit.

Mr Sandman seals eyes shut,
But not before he crawls in between my lids,
His sack of nightmares slung across his shoulders.
Which one will he choose tonight?

How Not to Write a Song

(The Kling Klang Klong Song)

Kouldachoungekouldachounge Kuoldachenko and
Pattatapatapattata Patong
Were sitting together one evening when they decided to write a
song.
Kouldachoungekouldachounge Kuoldachenko said to
Pattatapatapattata Patong
'Let's write a song together and have a puff on the bong.'

Oshimadoshi and Squishy McSquashy happened to come along.
They walked up to the front door, they rang on the bell, ding
dong.
Oshimadoshi and Squishy McSquashy, recently home from Hong
Kong,
Were surprised when the door was opened by Pattata in nought
but a thong.

Said Oshimadoshi to Squishy McSquashy 'Whatever they're
smoking, it's strong.'
Said Squishy McSquashy to Oshimadoshi 'You're right and it don't
'alf pong.'
Said Pattatapatapattata to Squishy and Oshi 'Do you fancy a cup
of Oolong?'
Kouldachoungekouldachounge piped up and said 'Why don't you
put on a sarong?'

Said Kouldachenko to Oshi 'My wiffy is squiffy but she's written the words for a song.

They're all wishy washy, a load of old tosh' he said 'Every word a diphthong.'

'O.K., so they're iffy, but even when squiffy, your wiffy is still well chong.

I'd hate to upset her so what could be better than if we all had a nice sing-along.'

Kling klang kling klang kling klang kling klang

Kling klang kling klang klong

Kling klang kling klang kling klang kling klang

Kling klang kling klang klong

Kling klang kling klang kling klang kling klang

Kling klang kling klang klong

Kling klang kling klang kling klang kling klang

Kling klang kling klang klong

The Nibbling Sea

Linda was a lovely girl, lived in a party world,

All of a jig and whirl, ribbon, bow and lace.

Happy as a summer's day, not one thought or curl astray,

Run to fun with no delay, to schoolgirl scenes and dreams.

Loved her Mum, her Dad and Sis, Granny, Gramps and Auntie Fliss,

Said her 'thank yous' with a kiss and beamed her toothy smile.

'I like sugar, I like tea, I like Mary in with me'

Skipping along from game to game,

Running home to Mum in the pouring rain.

'One potato, two potato, three potato four.'

Knocking breathlessly at the door.

Dip dip sky blue, who's it?

You?

And then one day, such a fun day,

A first ever trip to the sea - to the coast.

Such happiness, a family dream come true.

A neat and tidy B&B.

Air to breath, the ozone's free.

Mum doesn't have to cook,

Dad doesn't have to wash up, or Linda to dry.

Sandwiches for dinner, fish and chips for tea.

'Watch out for the seagulls!'
Coffee for Mum, beer for Dad and milk-shakes.
Banana, strawberry, chocolate ...... so many flavours!
There's ice cream melting under a grinning sun,
Roundabout rides, crazy golf, fishing nets and li-los.
Penny arcades, buckets and spades, plastic flags for sandcastles.

And the beach.
Always the beach.

Run giggling from the greedy tide.
Skip around the slimy seaweed.
Salt between red toes.
'I know! Let's go for a walk on the cliffs.'
Sparkling sea from the green chalky, land.
'How's that for a view?'
A distant, hazy horizon and the endless beyond.

Just a short walk.
A simple walk, a simple pleasure.
A walk to sudden, horrific death.
A cliff edge, enticing, deceitful.
Crumbling.
Retreating land betrays, gives way to an envious, implacable rival.
The ever nibbling sea.

And the waves crashed on the ally ally ooh.

And mother earth said 'this will never never do.'

And drops Linda to her doom, a ragged Looby Loo.

A moment of jealous petulance, plunging Linda into nightmare terror.

Into Never Ever Land.

Dip dip sky blue.

Who's it? Yes! You!

5 potatoes 6 potatoes 7 potatoes more.

Linda falls from land to sea, falls screaming through death's door.

A Certain Sadness

Come to think of it, the weather was ideal.
Dull, dreary,
Occasional stair rods,
The odd ray of sunshine.
Apposite.

Looking back, from the wharf,
to the bridge
And along to the tower.
As good a place as any.
Maybe better.

One last entry into The Ledger.
The last swallow.
London Pride and chips
Should old acquaintance etc.
Who knows?

The Doorstep Sidestep

A doorstep quickstep.

Standing on ceremony.

First step.

A journey.

To another country.

An odyssey newly begun.

Right magic wrong spell, truth to tell.

Perhaps never to be told.

A doorstep sidestep.

A separation of weft from waft.

A denial.

Faint heart.

Wasteful in consequence.

A step change.

A secret to be revealed.

Or kept forever.

Wept over.

They crept slowly up the stairs
To catch their futures unawares.
She opened the doors of the ark
And instantly let in the dark.

The Doolally Tap

Uncle Jack, Uncle Jack,
Is it true what Mummy says, your mind is cracked?
Uncle Jack,
Is it true what Mummy says, they turned their backs?

Uncle Jack,
Is it true what Daddy says, I must beware?
Uncle Jack, Uncle Jack,
Is it true what Daddy says, I must take care?

The man who lives up the stairs.
Creeps up on you unawares.
Striped pyjamas, worn threadbare.
He grunts and gives you such a scare.

Diary days of sun-kissed boredom.
Brain frazzled by an Indian sun.
Discharged, shipped back to Scotland,
A sanatorium cold and grey.
No more swimming, no more painting,
No more walking miles a day – you were simply thrown away
Before rescued by the last in line
To work amongst the flesh and blood.

The raw skin.
The gristle and the bone.
The sweetbreads of heaven, with no redemption.
A butchered carcass, all alone.

Round the bend, round the twist.
Hardly able to make a fist of this life.
Did you take the rap for The Doolally Tap?
You certainly took the blame – made the walk of shame.

The man who tinkers with his Shadow.
Cross the road, avoid the fellow.
The neighbours think he's strange, he's odd.
A bit unhinged, and a grumpy sod.

Uncle Jack, Uncle Jack,
Is it true what I've been told, you got the sack?
Uncle Jack,
Is it true what they all say, you're not intact?

Uncle Jack,
Is it true what I've been told, you're in disgrace?
Uncle Jack, Uncle Jack,
Is it true what I've been told in whispered haste?

Seven Shades of Isolation

Monday's Children are feeling great
They've been walking around the family estate

Tuesday's Children have their feet in the foam
They've escaped to their holiday home

Wednesday's Children have no reason to grouse
There is much to do in their comfortable house

Thursday's Children are running to fat
One Mum and three kids, stuck in a flat

Friday's Children rest on a stone cold bed
They have no roof to cover their head

Saturday's Children are harder to find
Slowly but surely losing their mind

Sunday's Children, be they poor or rich
Are two metres distant, in a sexton's ditch

Hangman's Gulch

They're taking me down to Hangman's Gulch
Where the gibbet creaks and the sulking Vultures
Watch Death arriving at breakneck speed
And the witches waiting to gather my seed.

They'll bury me down by Deadman's Creek,
The resting place of the flawed and the weak,
Where no sweetheart will come to weep at my grave
And no angels will come my soul to save.

They've booked my passage across The Styx
Where a drooling Cerberus patiently sits
To fast track me down to Circle 10
And my own special corner in Satan's Den

Forever I'll languish in Paimon's pavilion,
Forever and always consigned to oblivion,
For there is nothing that passes as fast as a bier
And nothing that dries as swift as a tear.

Timed out

Sincerity, dripping like saliva from a minister's mealy mouth.

A complacent chewing as though death is something to savour.

Unhelpful platitudes.

Mumbled prayers.

Hymns ground out with embarrassment.

Mourners surrounding a box -

Acquaintances mostly.

A smattering of colleagues,

No family to speak of.

A jumble of grey, begrudged flowers.

Shoes splashed with rain and dirt.

Door keys fingered in pockets,

Chilled flesh and damp bone clasping logo invested umbrellas.

Is he gazing down from heaven?

Is he looking up from below?

In the DMZ perhaps?

Or absorbed into oblivion?

Not reincarnated?

Surely 'Been there, done that' must apply?

Once is enough for anyone.

And when all the mumblings and embarrassments are done with.

When the tea and coffee has been drunk, the beer quaffed and the wine sipped

And memories have been shared,

We take our solemn leave.

We scuttle gratefully home to place our door keys in their locks,

Our umbrellas in their stands and wrench off our dirty shoes,

Interring death in a place that is quieter than any grave.

Michaela

Cry out Michaela, cry for me.
A summer dress but cold as you can be.
Damp grass beneath a shady tree.
Cry out Michaela, cry for me.

A body over exposed.
Arms askew.
Buckled red sandals,
White socks, stained green,
Stained red.

Shout out Michaela, shout to me.
Such prettiness, but bleeding to concede
Death to frantic ecstasy.
Shout out Michaela, shout at me.

Seed of Onan come into bloom,
Stale in the scuffled dirt.
Fear stained cardigan -
Torn pink skin
Where life begged for mercy.
But mercy favoured need.
Sweet fairytale of life stamped out.

Strike out Michaela, strike at me.

Oblivion will set us free.

And the world will forget our agonies.

Strike out Michaela ...

The Revenge of Montezuma

It was a dreary sort of Saturday, I was out shopping with the wife.

Trailing in and trailing out, not a single purchase made.

It's no wonder there are troubles in the High Street retail trade.

 On the previous evening I had been out with my mates.

A beer or two, a couple more, a normal Friday night.

And, as per usual, the munchies arrived, so off we went for a bite.

A Chinese, the chippy or a burger bar, we knew none would hit the spot.

So a curry it was, as it always is and I had a vindaloo

Not for one moment thinking of the terrible things it might do.

We were in M&S, my trouble and strife rifling through the sale rail,

When I suddenly realised, to my chagrin, I'd developed an urgent need.

No doubt brought on, I said to myself, as a result of last night's feed.

So, clenching my cheeks and forcing a smile, I said 'I have to pay a visit.

I shan't be long, so you carry on, I'll meet you in the cafe.'

With sweat on my brow and complaining bowels, I swiftly scuttled away.

I thanked my stars and the heavens above there were facilities close to hand.

Through the bras and knickers I rushed in eager anticipation.

I saw the signs, I followed the arrows, I found the door to my salvation.

Desperate now, I barged my way in, trap number 2 was empty.

Sweet relief - just in time - but vital equipment was missing.

Curses, 'Merde', as the French do say 'Ou est le papier?'

My belly was gurgling and griping, this wasn't over yet.

My emissions, excessive, broke EU law, noxious, toxic fumes.

Deadly pollutants poisoning the air, preceded by sonic booms.

I sat on my throne, splitter splat, my callards around my ankles.

I began to feel queasy, sweaty and sick, and the spices were starting to sting.

Expletive deleted, things couldn't get worse.

Then I heard the fire alarm ring.

The Valetudinarian

A pinprick of a spark escapes from oblivion,

Spat into existence with pain, love and disregard.

Ignorant of time gone by and time to come.

Flickering, spluttering, occasionally bursting into flame,

Before a final guttering.

A last tiny, diminished smut, sucked crumbling through the crack between the evening and the night.

Fading into the wrong side of the sunset.

Why Else?

For the love of god
I think not
For the love of life
Almost certainly not
For the love of money
I hope not
For the love of country
Don't be silly
For the love of the game
Perhaps
For the love of a child
That's for them to decide
For the love of you
Why else?